JOHN GOTTI

The Teflon Don of the Gambino Crime Family

Walter Barnes

TABLE OF CONTENTS

JOHN GOTTI:
THE LAST OF THE GODFATHERS

Some people are destined for great things. Other people are destined to become legends, though not in the way that most childhood dreams are conceived. John Joseph Gotti was a man with fortitude, intelligence, innovation, and style. He was also a murderer, committed many atrocities, and made no apologies for his actions. A mobster through and through, his life was consumed with the desire for material wealth and power.

Gotti was not a morally sound man and never made any illusions of a sanctimonious nature. He used his intelligence and cunning for his own hedonism. His need to ensure his own comfort and legacy trumped any morals. His first loves were power and gambling, though he was notoriously a terrible gambler. Known as "Dapper Don" for his love of designer suits, and "Teflon Don," for the inability to have legal charges stick, he truly was a prototypical mafia boss. He seemed to have no fear of legal repercussions and when finally brought to justice he simply stated, "I'm a man's man, and I'm ready to take my medicine." Most associates of the mob refer to their paths as "the life." John Gotti lived this life of crime, money, and power to its fullest, and wouldn't let anything or anyone stop him.

HOODLUM DREAMER

John Joseph Gotti Jr. was born on October 27, 1940 in the South Bronx, NY to Italian immigrant parents, John Gotti Sr. and Philomena Gotti. He was the fifth of thirteen children. Gott's start in life was in no way like the flashy lifestyle he would one day obtain. John Gotti Sr. was a day laborer who earned a meager wage, in addition to having a heavy gambling problem. The family moved often, and his childhood was extremely poverty stricken. John Gotti Jr.'s resentment for his father is obvious. "The guy never worked a [explicative] day in his life. He was a rolling stone; he never provided for the family. He never did nothin'. He never earned nothin'. And we never had nothin'." He blamed his father for the family being trapped in poverty, and at an early age he vowed to do something different.

After several moves due to his father's inconsistent salary, he ended up in east New York, in Brooklyn, at the beginning of his adolescence. This was a delicate age and where Gotti was first exposed to the mafia lifestyle. These men were the opposite of everything he despised in his father. They had nice clothes, cars, and their families wanted for nothing materially. Gotti was hooked and began chasing the "mafia dream." Around age twelve he started running errands for the local mob, Cosa Nostra (a catch-all name for his generation's mob based in Sicily), and was soon known for his "tough" reputation. In the mafia world, this is considered valuable and he became the unofficial leader of an adolescent gang. Even at this age, he had a penchant for mischief.

Known for street fighting and stealing, his name soon became the fear of many youths. After committing many petty crimes, he had his first law enforcement run-in at the tender age of fourteen. During an attempted robbery of a cement-mixing machine, his feet became stuck and crushed under the mixer. Not only was he arrested, this accident left him with a noticeable gait for the rest of his life. This gait, as well as his penchant for violence, would follow him for his entire life.

Gotti was attracted to "coffee clubs" where mafia men frequented. It was here that he became close to the owner of one of these clubs, Carmine Fatico. Fatico ran the Ozark Park Boys. At this point, the Gambino family was not in power and the family was dominated by the Anastasia family, run by Albert Anastasia. The Gambino family would take over in 1957, after Anastasia was allegedly murdered by Carlo Gambino, his successor.

Gotti worked closely with Fatico. He was entrusted with more and more high-paying and dangerous gigs. It was during these formative years that he also met Aniello Dellocroce, who would continue to be his mentor as the Gambino family began to take shape. Dellocroce inspired Gotti as a sort of father figure to mimic. Albert Anastasia and Carlo Gambino, with their power and grandeur, were idols to worship. At age sixteen, he dropped out of Franklin K. Lane High School and small-time crime, officially joining the Fulton-Rockaway gang. He soon cemented himself as the leader within this group as well. His petty crime youth days were over. He was now in serious mob territory.

It was here that he met Angello Ruggerio, the talkative nephew of Dellocroce, who would continue to be a lifelong associate. Once he reached the end of his teen years, he was already considered a low-level henchman in Fatico's gang. From 1958 to1966, Gotti was arrested many times for a myriad of things: gun possession, burglaries, street fighting; and as he aged the crimes became more dangerous and severe.

His whatever-it-takes, "ruthless" reputation caught the eye of higher up associates in Cosa Nostra. Gotti and an amateur boxer named Wilfred Johnson, or "Willie Boy," were instructed to show the family's brawn and strength to a used car dealer that dared to break up a stolen car ring. Both were not small men. Gotti, at 5,10" had a muscular build and Willie, the physique of a boxer. The car salesman barely survived the beating. Gotti's name and its infamous cutthroat legacy was now catching the attention of many in the future Gambino mob. A foreshadowing to his inevitable rise began to take shape.

"The Crew"- Meet the Mob

There were many people that would ride with Gotti to the eventual top of the Cosa Nostra. Five associates worth noting are: Aniello Dellacroce, Angelo Ruggerio, Wilfred "Willie Boy" Johnson, Frank Locascio, and Sammy "The Bull" Gravano. All played a very vital role in the rise and downfall of John Gotti's infamous mob career.

Aniello Dellacroce was a traditional mafia gangster who followed and served as underboss for many different mafia "godfathers." He worked under: Albert Anastasia, Carlos Gambino, Paul Castellano, to eventually John Gotti. Many think that Gotti's rise would have not been possible without Dellacroce. His unique character was obvious. He often dressed as a priest to deter attention away from authorities with the pseudo-name of Father O'Neil. He hated police officers and would often taunt and even target them without fear. A ruthless killer, many called him evil and dangerous. Some reported that he had the eyes of a killer and was one of the most feared men in the family. He was still a loyal man despite his evident lack of morality, and though his mentor, Albert Anastasia, was presumably shot dead by Carlos Gambino, he stayed loyal to the family and continued his duties under Gambino. He was always a faithful underboss despite many changings of arms. He even tried to keep the peace amongst factions when Paul Castellano was picked over him for head boss.

Angelo Ruggerio was a man without a conscience or a muzzle. Nicknamed "Quack Quack" for his tendency for endless chatter and a strange waddle gait due to a foot condition, he was not the most popular mob man. Many suspected him of having several undiagnosed mental illnesses. He had no filter and would tell any of his complaints about his superiors, or talk about the family's plans to anyone who would listen. This nondiscretionary behavior does not work in the mob business but was the authorities' dream. He was wire-tapped countless times, laying out dozens of mob secrets throughout his career, his thick, smoke-laden voice always recognizable on tapes. Strangely, in addition to being violent and frightening, he once threatened to feed his enemies to man-eating sharks he claimed to have in a pool, and also once foolishly threatened to kill an F.B.I. agent. A morbidly obese and delusional man, his ego was bigger than life as well. Many wanted to get rid of him and considered him a nuisance if not an extreme threat. The only reason he was never killed was due to the protection of his uncle, Dellacroce. Ruggerio was a huge contributor to Gotti and other mafia men's downfall. Gotti eventually disowned him for his loud mouth, as his recordings were used to put his brother Gene in prison. When Ruggerio died from lung cancer in 1989, Gotti did not even attend his funeral.

Wilfred "Willie Boy" Johnson had a rocky if not sad life with the mob and as a F.B.I. informant. His mother was Native American and his father Italian, making him a "half breed," and unable to become a made man. Willie resented being treated like an underling in the family. This kind of treatment was highlighted even further after being arrested for a mob-related crime and his family not being taken care of while he was in jail, despite a promise from Fatico that he would do so. His family was forced to go on welfare. This and other reasons are what lead him to eventually become an informant in 1967. Though he gave up information on many different mob men, hide-outs, and plans, he was often hesitant to completely give up his "friend," Gotti. They had been close since their teenage days and Johnson still had some loyalty. In a move to try and push Johnson to testify against Gotti, a prosecutor released his informant status in court. He was offered a space in the witness protection program if he testified, but he refused. Like most discovered "snitches" in the mob, he was killed in 1988, gunned down right outside his home by another family, the Bonnaoos. The act was intended as a favor to the rising Gotti.

Frank Locascio , like Gotti, was also born to first generation Italian immigrant parents in New York. He became a made man fairly early in the late 1950s and was a trusted Gambino mob member. He was acting underboss at one point when another mob member went to prison, but held the official title as head capo under the underboss, Sammy Gravano. He was often Gotti's right hand man during his reign. He was cold, calculating, and mostly loyal to Gotti. The only time he started to wane is after Gotti started to act erratically in prison, right before the 1992 trial. Eventually he and Sammy made a pact to kill Gotti if they were ever released. This never happened for Locascio. He still sits in prison and has no projected release date.

Sammy "The Bull" Gravano was one of the main contributors of Gotti's downfall. He earned his nickname at the young age of thirteen when he beat up several young men trying to steal his bike. Local mafia men remarked that he "fought like a bull." He disliked Paul Castellano after a property dispute and made it known that he would have no trouble turning against him if necessary. He was heavily involved in the coup to kill Castellano. He was an underboss for Gotti and supported him until the 1992 trial. He eventually turned against him after hearing Gotti on tape trying to pin him for the murder cases brought against them by the district attorney. He went on the stand and ratted Gotti out as the mafia boss and mastermind. He was put in the witness protection program after a very short prison sentence but was booked again in 2000 for a massive drug ring in Arizona. He was released is 2017 and is still alive and free.

Family Life:
Growing Up Gotti

G otti's family life timeline differed greatly from that of his professional crime life. He almost led a double life—one as a hardened criminal, the other in an effort to be a family man. This timeline showcases Gotti's unique personality.

Though his love of money and power was huge, after meeting his wife in 1958, his attitude temporarily changed. After marrying Victoria DiGiorgio in 1962, he tried to remove himself from the crime world. It may have been a push from his new young bride or the cries of his first child, Angel, but he tried to work outside of his mob life for a few years. He took work as a coat presser and an assistant truck driver. A "legit" life proved to be about as fruitful as his father's efforts. The pull of potential power and money was too great and he went back to "the life."

His daughter, Victoria, was born soon after Angel and an anecdote on how Gotti could not pay the hospital bill showed his brazenness. The hospital told him flatly that he could bring his wife and daughter home when he could pay his bill. John instead removed his newly labored wife and days-old daughter from the hospital in the middle of the night, like a prison break. He would often tell his daughter Victoria fondly, years later, that they bonded that night.

He would go on to have five children with DiGiorgio: Angel, Victoria, John Jr., Frank (who did not survive to adulthood) and Peter. His children fondly remember their very early years with their father as pleasant when they were ignorant of his profession. They saw him as a funny, gregarious father who could often have the excitement of a child. Though they were happy in the beginning, they were also largely unaware of how poor they were and how their parents struggled. The family's entire income was reliant on their father's inconsistent mob life salary, coupled with Gotti's bad gambling habit which drained much of the funds. Gotti despised the poverty of his father, yet the cycle was repeated for a large part of his own children's childhood.

Victoria remembers her father being absent often, her mother struggling, and she and her siblings playing with boxes for toys. Her mother made their clothes and cut their own hair. The home was kept very traditional and often strict. The girls were discouraged from dating too early and all of their boyfriends were screened by Gotti. Their mother often resented her husband's mob life and their fighting was not infrequent. There were physical altercations between the parents and one instance where DiGiorgio stabbed Gotti.

Gotti was prideful and secretive. He tried as much as possible to shield his children from the realities of his work. He fabricated different jobs as a plumbing or construction contractor and time away was a "work trip." This started to unravel as his children aged and grew more aware. Even when sent to penitentiaries, Gotti continued his fabrications and would tell his children that he was at the prison doing plumbing/construction work. His daughter Victoria remembers the traumatic day she was made aware of her father's profession. In grade school around age seven, her classmates were doing reports on their heroes. Most chose their fathers. She did as well but as she was giving the report about her "construction contractor" dad who built "giant structures", another classmate called her father a jailbird in front of the entire class. She asked her mother and was told the truth. Victoria was devastated and had many anxieties after the incident, wondering about her and her family's safety. Her brother Peter remembers being relieved when he heard his dad snoring at night, knowing that he had made it home and not been killed.

They never lived in luxury, even when Gotti eventually became extremely wealthy. When they moved from Brooklyn to a modest four bedroom in Howard Beach, NY, Victoria said it "was like moving to Beverly Hills." Gotti had money management problems like his father and spent his money on gambling and flashy suits versus familial extravagance. His wife and children always maintained their "pious" working-class, Brooklyn background. Though as Gotti's fame grew their life did become more surreal. "The public saw my father right out of central casting. He looked the part, acted the part... he was the part! The real life Godfather," said Victoria. "People treat him like he was the second coming of Christ!" At her wedding, Victoria could sense the coming of something big. People were already treating him like the new mafia boss, and she remembers not knowing many of the guests. People were already revering Gotti as a Godfather.

CHANGES AND BECOMING CAPO

Fatico's Ozone Park crew eventually branched off into the Bergin Unit. They had a headquarters called *The Bergin Fish and Hunt Club,* disguised as a non-profit. Gotti was successful as a criminal; lorry hijacking and murder were his "specialties." His unit was used along with other sects to hijack many types of expensive cargo at John F. Kennedy Airport (formally Idlewild Airport). This type of crime, at a federal base, shows the bravado and fearlessness that would soon immortalize Gotti. His childhood friend, Ruggerio, was also a perpetrator. The F.B.I. started following the young mafia entrepreneur and associates at their criminal base. Gotti was first arrested in 1968, after a United Airlines employee identified him signing for stolen goods. Not two months out on bail, he was arrested again for stealing a cigarette truck worth $50,000 near the New Jersey Turnpike. Additional hijacking charges from a previous job were discovered and the charges all added up to his first real stint in prison. Gotti and Ruggerio were handed a three-year sentence.

Like many mafia inmates, his time served only grew his status and connections. It also gave him even more respect for not snitching and staying loyal to the mob. He was now considered a valuable member of the Bergin Unit. While he was in prison, his capo, Fatico, ran into legal trouble. He had to lay low and avoid criminal activity.

Fatico named Gotti as acting capo. This was perfect timing for Gotti. He was now working directly for his mentor, Dellacroce, the underboss in the now Gambino family. Gotti was in deep in the mob and determined to "make it big."

Events transpired to further test Gotti's loyalty. Gambino's nephew, Emmanuel Gambino, had been murdered. It was up to Gotti, his old friend Ruggerio, and another unnamed associate to reciprocate the violence. They were ordered to kill James McBratney, one of the perpetrators of his nephew's abduction and murder. Gotti finally had the chance to prove himself in a big way, though his skills in discretion were not yet perfected. James McBratney was accosted at a bar by "undercover agents." They were, in fact, Gotti, Ruggerio and another man in disguise. They tried to persuade McBratney to go with them, and when he refused he was shot dead in front of many witnesses. The desire to get the job done and prove himself to Gambino trumped any sort of discretion.

Gotti and Ruggerio were identified quickly by witnesses in a line-up. The other associate was not discovered. Though he was facing serious time, Gotti never seemed afraid of spending time in jail. With Gambino's connections, he secured Roy Cohn, an infamous lawyer who frequently helped rich, powerful men dodge prison time. Cohn was able to fenagle a reduced sentence with an attempted manslaughter plea. For the murder, Gotti got an anemic four years but only served two. In addition, while he was in custody, guards were paid to take Gotti to secret meetings with his relatives and mafia family. The perks of performing for the head boss were obvious.

A Made Man

otti did not get to bask in Gambino's favor for very long. In 1976, while he was still in prison, Gambino died of heart complications at the age of seventy-four. Rather than name his expected heir, Dellacroce, as the new head boss, Gambino left the position to Paul Castellano, his son-in-law. Castellano was a more "modern gangster" and wanted to focus more on white-collar crime, while Dellacroce, Gotti, and many of their associates were traditionalists focusing on loan-sharking, hijacking, and drug-dealing. One of Paul Castellano's biggest rules was forbidding any kind of drug trafficking. He believed the long sentences could persuade family members to become informants. This did not sit well with Gotti, as he and others had amassed a hugely profitable heroin trafficking ring. They ignored Castellano's law and defiantly continued their business.

In 1977, Gotti finally became "made man," meaning he was officially in the mob. He was also made head capo, or *consigliere*. As a head capo, Gotti's gambling habit intensified. Many of his inferiors and colleagues complained about the exuberant amount of money wasted weekly. Such grand sums as a $60,000 loss in one dice game were reported. Gotti was not a successful gambler, and while he often ran fruitful gambling dens, he himself, more often than not, was the loser. This would impact some of his associate's salaries. Still, he was beginning to amass more wealth and notoriety. People revered and respected him.

Just as his professional crime life was becoming successful, tragedy struck. While riding a mini-bike in their neighborhood, his son Frank, then twelve-years old, was hit and killed by Gotti's neighbor, John Farvara. Gotti's wife Victoria was devastated and attempted suicide several times. Farvara tried to come over and formally apologize to the Gotti family but was screamed at and physically assaulted by Victoria. Gotti did not forgive this accident. He whisked his family away on a vacation to Florida and during this time, Farvara disappeared. While it was never proven, it was believed Gotti ordered a hit on Farvara. He was never seen or heard from again and was rumored to have died in a pit of acid. Gotti's ruthless reputation showed that he had no scruples in getting even when someone crossed him. There was no room for mistakes in his ego-centric world.

After he became head capo under Dellocroce, his responsibilities, criminal activity, and attention from the feds all became elevated. In an effort to prosecute on loan sharking and gambling, a wiretap was installed at Gotti's Bergen Unit. Gotti didn't seem to fear these wiretaps at first, though he did fear backlash when he heard himself bash his mentor Dellacroce in some of the tapes. He even seemed to show remorse in trash-talking his mentor. The taped also showed the strictness and fury that Gotti displayed as he ruled over the club with his younger brother Gene and Ruggerio as underlings. The stakeout revealed a huge gambling organization, but Gotti and his associates were somehow untouched. Regardless, the feds were tireless in their effort to bring up charges against different mob families and continued their efforts.

DISSENT AND MAKING A MURDER

B y 1985, over fifty mafia members had different racketeering and narcotic distribution charges. Castellano and Dellcroce were among some of the men charged. Gotti and again Dellacroce were also indicted on racketeering charges, but the charges were dismissed after fear that some key F.B.I. informants would be discovered during the trial. Prosecutors continued to bring up charges such as racketeering or loan sharking, and Gotti seemed to always dodge the prison cell. Other mob members would fall around him but Gotti would continually fall between the cracks.

As all these cases were proliferating, serious allegations and charges were brought up against Ruggerio and Gene Gotti. They were indicted for heroin trafficking. This was blatant disobedience against Castellano's law, and the penalty was death. The feds claimed they had taped evidence that Ruggerio was the dealer, and Castellano wanted to hear the tape. Ruggerio knew that if Castellano got his hands on the tape, his death note would be signed. Gotti, not interested in his brother Gene getting murdered in addition to having a hand in the trafficking ring, chose Ruggerio's side.

Ruggerio pleaded with his Uncle Dellacroce, as the loyal underboss, to intervene and help their crew escape Castellano. For a short time Dellacroce played mediator and tried to keep the peace, but two growing factions were reaching a breaking point. They met at Dellacroce's home, where another wiretap overheard their dilemma. "I've been tryin' to take your part with these tapes from the very, very beginning ... Then all we gotta do then, we go and roll it up and go to war," Dellacroce told Ruggiero on one of the tapes. Meaning Dellacroce knew that if the tape was discovered by Castellano, a war would ensue. Gotti, Ruggerio and many other associates were poised and ready for a takeover. Their faction and support had continued to grow by traditionists that supported the old ways. Dellacroce could not play mediator for very long.

Dellacroce died of brain cancer in 1985. Gotti was heartbroken that his "mob father" and mentor was gone. Castellano had begun to resent and turn against Dellacroce due to his siding with Ruggerio and Gotti; in a move deemed unforgivable by Gotti, Castellano did not attend Dellacroce's funeral. Also, once Gotti found out that the government was following their drug activities, he did not trust Castellano to not indict him and his associates. Gotti's plot to get revenge began to take shape. He was ready to pounce on the mafia king's throne to ensure he and his associates were safe.

On December 1985, a cold evening near Christmas day, Castellano exited his limo to enter Sparks Steakhouse in midtown New York and was shot multiple times. he. Gotti sat in a nearby parked car and used walkie talkies to communicate with the gunman. The four hit men were dressed in white trench coats and Russian hats. Not only did they kill Castellano, but they arranged the killing of his close associates, or anyone they felt would question Gotti's right of passage to mob boss. Castellano was shot first, and then Biotti, his right-hand man, was shot directly after him as he exited the vehicle. Robert DiBernardo and Liborio Milito, Gambino's associates, were lured into meetings and shot in the head. It was a coup.

THE GODFATHER DAYS

A few days after the murder, the first meeting of the new Gambino family took place at Caesar's Restaurant. Joseph Gallo, the family's counselor, presided over the meeting. Gotti and his crew all stood stoic and threatening, holding guns during the meeting, mainly for intimidation purposes. Though the changing of mafia bosses was historically married with murder, Gotti and his associates were not eager to admit or brag about their act. According to the commission of mob rules, the penalty for killing a boss was also death. Though many associates suspected Gotti, their intimidation tactics worked and no one questioned their crew. After Castellano's funeral, a meeting was held several weeks later with Gambino and high profile members to discuss, nominate, and appoint a new head boss. An associate named Frankie DiCicco nominated Gotti, and others followed suit. Approval for the new boss was sent to the other mafia families and they all agreed on the choice, with a warning that whomever shot Castellano would eventually be brought to justice. Within weeks, Gotti was the new mafia boss. Sammy Gravano was appointed the new underboss, with Frank Lucerio under him. Gotti did not get to enjoy his success for very long.

A case was ready for trial involving Romual Piecyk, a refrigerator repairman who claimed Gotti slapped him and stole $325 from him during a fight about a parking spot. Though the accusations were not serious, the trial was still a nuisance. Gotti's associates took care of it through intimidation and on the stand, Piecyk suddenly could not identify Gotti. Again, Gotti did not get to relax for very long. The feds brought up serious charges in Brooklyn involving racketeering. Gotti was on the line as well as his brother Gene and five other defendants. The case dragged on for nearly seven months, with over thirty hours of audio tapes and ninety witnesses. It was no match for the powerful, former district attorney Gotti and his crew had as their lawyer. Their lawyer claimed the tapes to be reaching and circumstantial. Despite the feds carefully crafted case, they were no match for Gotti's lawyer. A jury acquitted Gotti and his associates on all counts.

The Justice Department was mortified. The media officially named him "Teflon Don" and his celebrity grew. He finally had the money and extravagance that he so envied as a young man. This was hard to believe as the suits he would wear were valued between $2,000 and $3,000. Once his many trials began, he would infamously change suits during recess to "keep fresh." This would earn him the additional nickname "Dapper Don." Teflon Don continued his reign. Though, in true mob fashion, it was later found that the jury had been "fixed" and some jurors were paid off.

When Gotti took over as head boss, the former Gambino crime family had 23 different units, like the Bergin Unit, and he brought in over $500 million annually. Other mob families began to fall due to Federal interventions, but Gotti's mob remained strong. Gotti's cut was $10 million a year. His declared income was $100 thousand a year as a plumbing contractor. Gotti was not shy in spending his money. He bought a $300 thousand mountain vacation home in the Poconos and put the deed in his son's name to avoid the feds. He bought a cigarette boat and would often drive it around Sheepshead Bay, Brooklyn. He had fast cars, flashy cars, and dined at the most exclusive and expensive establishments, though he was always careful and often wary. A mob boss's life is almost always filled with envy and associates eager to take their position. He would always take tables close to walls while eating, facing the door.

Although he was a ruthless, violent person, many in his community loved him. He was generous, throwing many extravagant parties, including an annual Fourth of July party for the neighborhood. Because he grew up in poverty and worked his way to the top, many working class people respected and revered him. His easily approachable attitude and friendliness also contributed to his popularity. He was down to earth and talked and joked easily with reporters and even law enforcement officials. His air of confidence seemed impenetrable. He was able to afford some of the most powerful attorneys, and the feds couldn't touch him. He would bring an era of decadence and celebrity that rivaled any former boss.

Yet another trial was brought up in 1989, this time for ordering an assault. He was accused of ordering an assault on a labor union official, John O'Connell. O'Connell had been threatening to Gotti after snubbing his union, and Gotti reciprocated. Authorities had Gotti on tape bragging about how he was going to "rough this guy up." Incredulously, despite this evidence, Gotti was acquitted once again. Later it was found that this trial had been rigged as well. Gotti seemed to be untouchable. The media loved the acquittals as it made his mythological power a compelling story. The public loved the lure and romance of the mob life as it had been portrayed by Hollywood. Unfortunately for Gotti, this was his real life and he was about the get his comeuppance.

The Teflon Becomes Velcro

B y the time his final court case came around, Gotti felt untouchable. He had the media laughing along with him against the feds and was flying high. By this time as Don, he said goodbye to his Bergin haunt and mostly spent his time at the Ravenite Social Club. This is where he was arrested in 1990, along with Gravano and **Frank Locascio**. After being arrested, Gotti allegedly told the cops, "I bet you three to one I beat this." He never was a good gambler.

Not only did the feds have him fingered for the murders of Castellano, Bilotti, DiBernardo, Liborio Milito and Louis DiBono, they had him on a myriad of other charges as well, including: loan sharking, conspiracy to murder, racketeering, bribery, and tax evasion. Gotti was sinking. What's worse, his associate, Sammy "The Bull" Gravano turned against in him in plea bargain. The feds had countless hours of tapes, portions of which they played for Gravano, that contained dialogue where Gotti spoke ill of him and claimed he was responsible for the murders. Gotti's gossip and blame, similar to how he spoke about Dellacroce years ago, was one of his biggest undoings. Gravano turned and testified against him. This was the most damaging evidence and what nailed Gotti's coffin—a witness working close with Gotti, describing every illegal activity in detail. Gotti did not have much of a case. All of

Gotti's witnesses were dismissed as irrelevant and the only one left was his tax advisor. Gotti, usually calm and confident in court, began to lose his cool. He screamed at Gravano, calling him a "junkie," and ironically said this jury was fixed, making a metaphor to the 1919 World series.

The Teflon Don was done. It only took jurors fourteen hours to find Gotti and Locascio guilty on all counts. The prosecution quoted this to the media, "The Teflon is gone. The don is covered with Velcro, and all the charges stuck." Gotti was sentenced to life without the possibility of parole. His final appeal was overturned in 1994. This Dapper Don would switch his designer swag for an eternity of garish orange jumpsuits.

ENDGAME

In prison, he did not manage to keep out of trouble. In 1996, he was assaulted by another inmate, Walter Johnson, who claimed Gotti had called him a racial slur. There are rumors that Gotti conferred with the Aryan brotherhood to order a hit on Johnson, but others deny this claim. They state that Gotti hung out with mostly Latino and African American inmates, with no racial bias. He also was rumored to put a hit out on Locascio after he suspected him of siding with Gravano. Eventually, due to his confrontations, he was kept in solitary confinement. Though he tried to maintain his boss title while in prison by relaying commands to his brother Peter and son John Jr., this proved to be difficult. By 1998, his son was known to be the new head boss. It seemed the golden years were over. So many of Gotti's associates had been imprisoned and the family was significantly weaker. His wife was angry at the notion of her sons being involved in the mob and blamed Gotti.

His final prison days were in no way glamorous. He was kept in solitary confinement 23 hours a day. His daughter and wife, the Victorias, consistently rallied against the "cruel" treatment Gotti received. Surprisingly it didn't seem to break him psychologically. When his family or associates came to visit, he joked and was generally good natured. Though he was still moderately young, in his late 50s, his fast mob life of cigars and booze seemed to catch up with him. He was diagnosed with throat cancer and a tumor was removed in 1998. His appearance changed dramatically as he had to have part of his jaw removed and replaced with skin from other parts of his body. Always the comedian, he would joke with his wife Victoria, that he "didn't even have tits left."

In his final days his son, who had been given the title of head boss since his arrest in 1992, came for his blessing to leave the mob. John Jr. saw that most mafia men ended up shot or in a prison and he wanted to be a family man, present for his children. At first, Gotti Sr. was incredulous and angry, and chided him for having no pride, but eventually he understood and gave his blessing. Gotti died very soon after, on July 10, 2002. He died as many Dons and mafia men before him, in prison. Though Gotti's legacy will always be tainted with murder, torture and theft, he will be remembered, nonetheless. The need for infamy and power is usually what men like Gotti crave. Many refer to him as the last great Don. Gotti's "Godfather"-like qualities romanticized the mob and his reign still intrigues the public today.

ALL IN THE FAMILY:
THE GOTTI LEGACY

John Gotti was not the only Gotti to follow the mafia life. His influence amongst his siblings, and children is evident.

The Brothers:

Peter Gotti was probably the second most powerful, though was not as revered. He eventually became Don after Gotti Jr.'s resignation, but was referred to as "the dumbest Don." Though he started his mafia career at age twenty-one, he maintained a legit profession as a sanitation worker for many years. This might be why he was able to avoid jail time for so long. After an accident to his head, he retired with a disability pension at a fairly young age. He became a "made man" at age 49 and soon after the arrest and indictment of John A. Jr., he became acting boss. This did not last long and just a few days before his brother's death, he was indicted on racketeering charges. He was sentenced and a few years later was indicted again on money laundering and additional racketeering charges. He was sentenced to over twenty years and still sits in prison.

Richard V. Gotti:

Richard Gotti, born 1942, is still an acting capo in the Gambino crime family. He has a son, Richard G. Gotti, who is also in the Gambino family. His first arrest was for the violent crime of statutory rape in 1969. He had a legit job as a groundskeeper at Yankee Stadium as well as becoming a made man in the mafia by 1988. In 2002, the same year that John Gotti died, Richard was indicted on racketeering and extortion charges, with, strangely, the actor Steven Seagal as one of the defendants. He was sentenced to sixteen years in 2003 and was released from prison on August 12, 2005.

Gene Gotti:

Gene Gotti also became a made man in 1976 as an associate in the South Ozone Park crew. He would eventually become capo of this unit. In the early 1980s he ran a drug operation trafficking heroin. This was around the time Paul Castellano forbade any kind of drug trafficking, and resentment grew quickly. Gene was alongside his brother John during many arrests and trials. They looked after each other and helped each other grow each other's power within the mafia. Gene, much to his brother John's envy, was a successful gambler. He was involved with several murders but was never indicted, and met justice soon after. After two mistrials, Gene was sentenced to fifty years for running a heroin smuggling ring. He was imprisoned for twenty-nine years and released at the age of seventy-one on September 14, 2018. He is currently a capo.

Vincent Gotti:

Vincent Gotti was a drug user who was initially was banned from the mafia family. John looked at it as a potential security breach problem. His rationality was that drug users will often say and do anything to get their fix. In his youth and middle age, he was arrested several times for cocaine distribution, petty larceny and criminal impersonation. Eventually, after his brother John's death and Peter's rise, he became a made man in 2002. Soon after he became involved in loan sharking and ordered a failed hit on a Howard Beach bagel store owner. In 2008, he and others in the family were arrested and Vincent was charged with attempted murder. He received eight years and was released on February 22, 2015.

The Wife:

Victoria DiGiorgio:

Not much is known about Victoria DiGiorgio. She is alive at 77 and resides in Brooklyn. She has never really approved of the mob lifestyle and had many fights with her husband, especially involving her children and their mob involvement. She has been treated for depression many times, especially after her son Frank died. Many refer to her as an intelligent woman as well as a doting mother and grandmother.

The Kids:

Victoria Gotti:

One of the most well-known Gotti children, Victoria's life has not been bland. She married her high school sweetheart, Carmine Agnello, in 1984, much to her father's dismay. They had three sons: Carmine, Frank and John. Her husband was charged with extortion and arson in 2000. He spent nine years behind bars and was released in 2009. Victoria divorced him in 2003 with a hefty alimony of $12,500 a month. A writer, she reached commercial fame with her first book, *Women and Mitral Valve Prolapse*, about her own medical struggles. She published several other successful fiction books and memoirs. She and her sons reached American televisions with "Growing up Gotti", which aired from 2004 to 2005. In 2012, she was a contestant on

Donald Trump's Celebrity Apprentice. In 2016, her multi-million-dollar mansion was raided, based on an ongoing investigation.

Angel Gotti:

The eldest Gotti child, Angel is an avid supporter of her father and runs the Facebook page: *Shadow of My Father*. Always maintaining that their father was, in fact, a good man, she always defends and fights against bad rumors and press. She started a line of bejeweled flip flops but it has been obsolete since 2014. Her involvement in the mob is rumored but unknown.

John A. Gotti Jr.:

As acting mob boss from 1992 to 1999, "Junior", as he was known, was very similar to his father in many ways. During his time as the mafia boss he tried to learn from his father's mistakes and avoided wire talks and bugs as much as possible by conducting many meetings outside, while walking. Many found him inept though, and unlike his father, a poor negotiator. Some other gangs and crime families flatly refused to do any business with him. After the small amount of time he spent behind bars from 1999 to 2001; he gave up the title of boss, though just as father predicted, the feds did not leave him alone. He had four racketeering trials from 2004 to 2009, all ending in mistrials. Eventually the feds gave up, earning him the nickname "Teflon Jr." After the feds left him alone, he left the mob and focused on different business ventures, using his celebrity. An A&E special aired recently called, *Gotti: Godfather and Son*, which shows released footage from the father and son's last conversation in prison before John Gotti Sr.'s death. His son, John Gotti III, is a famous MMA boxer.

Peter Gotti:

Continuously protected and discouraged from entering the mob life as the youngest sibling, Peter was the only male Gotti child that avoided jail time. His son, also with the namesake of his late father, was not as lucky. He was found with over 200 oxycodone pills and $40 thousand in cash. He accepted a plea deal and was sentenced to eight years in 2017, at the young age of twenty-three.

Made in the USA
Middletown, DE
30 October 2023